How to Get Out of a Rut

Discover How to Shake Things Up and Flourish When You Find Yourself Stuck in a Rut

by Trish Meyers

Table of Contents

Introduction 1

Chapter 1: How to Figure out What You Want 7

Chapter 2: Shaking Things Up for Inspiration 11

Chapter 3: Connecting with Your Physical Self 15

Chapter 4: How to Practice Positive Thinking 19

Chapter 5: Marching Forward with Small Steps 23

Chapter 6: How to Be Accountable 27

Conclusion 31

Introduction

Almost everyone finds themselves in a rut at some point in life. While it is normal to experience periods of feeling stuck and unmotivated, it can also be quite disheartening. Being in a rut can mean different things to different people at different times in their lives. A rut can refer to one's work, relationships, or personal life. Or a rut could affect all these aspects of a person's life simultaneously. Whatever part of your life is being affected, a rut means that you are not living passionately. It means you are uninspired and unproductive, and things that you once enjoyed have become routine and tedious. Your days have begun to run together, so much so that each day feels exactly like the day before.

Being in a rut sometimes means that you are excruciatingly bored with your life, but you are unsure of how to change it. Or perhaps you have tried to change things, yet you were unable to shake the feeling of monotony. You might know the reason why you are in a rut. Perhaps you dislike your job or are unhappy in your relationship. In these instances, getting out of the rut is fairly straightforward. Changing jobs or ending your relationship would be obvious first steps in those scenarios. More often, however, the reason behind being in a rut isn't as clear. Maybe you have a good job, a loving spouse, and plenty of friends, but you still feel as if something is missing. In these cases, you will need to spend some time and energy determining the cause of your discontent.

Getting out of a rut does take a bit of hard work and perseverance, but it is definitely worth it. Being in a rut means you are not able to make progress, no matter how hard you work. You don't get any work done at the office, you don't make progress in your relationship, and you just can't lose those last ten pounds. Regardless of how much effort you put forth, your rut will prevent you from being successful. Even worse, the boredom and feeling of meaninglessness that accompanies a rut can lead to depression, which can in turn deplete one's motivation to break free from tedium. It is a vicious cycle, and it is something that occurs far too often in our modern-day society.

The good news is that with a bit of self-reflection and a lot of determination, you can break the cycle and get out of any rut. You *can* have an exciting and fulfilling life, you *can* wake up every morning eager to start your day, and you *can* approach each moment with enthusiasm and zeal. In the following chapters, we'll discuss some ideas that will help you get out of your rut and begin living a life you will truly love.

© Copyright 2014 by Miafn LLC - All rights reserved.

This document is geared towards providing reliable information in regards to the topic and issue covered. The publication is sold with the idea that the publisher is not required to render accounting, officially permitted, or otherwise, qualified services. If advice is necessary, legal or professional, a practiced individual in the profession should be ordered.

- From a Declaration of Principles which was accepted and approved equally by a Committee of the American Bar Association and a Committee of Publishers and Associations.

In no way is it legal to reproduce, duplicate, or transmit any part of this document in either electronic means or in printed format. Recording of this publication is strictly prohibited and any storage of this document is not allowed unless with written permission from the publisher. All rights reserved.

The information provided herein is stated to be truthful and consistent, in that any liability, in terms of inattention or otherwise, by any usage or abuse of any policies, processes, or directions contained within is solely and completely the responsibility of the recipient reader. Under no circumstances will any legal responsibility or blame be held against the publisher for any reparation, damages, or monetary loss due to the information herein, either directly or indirectly.

Respective authors own all copyrights not held by the publisher.

The information herein is offered for informational purposes solely, and is universal as so. The presentation of the information is without contract or any type of guarantee assurance.

The trademarks that are used are without any consent, and the publication of the trademark is without permission or backing by the trademark owner. All trademarks and brands within this book are for clarifying purposes only and are the owned by the owners themselves, not affiliated with this document.

Chapter 1: How to Figure out What You Want

If you want to get out of your rut, you will need to figure out what you really want from life. What really matters to you? Is your large expensive home worth the weekly sixty hours of mind-numbing office work? Or would you rather move to a smaller home and take a lower-paying job that you love? Are you staying in your relationship because it makes you happy, or because it would be too troublesome to break it off? Too often we move through life striving to meet goals set by someone else—our parents, our significant others, society, etc. We are expected to go to school, get a high-paying job, buy a nice house, fill our nice house with stylish things, get married, have children, and so on. It is as if we are set to autopilot, and that is a surefire way to end up in a rut. Rather than automatically doing what you think is expected of you, take time to think about the trajectory of your life. Ask yourself whether the actions you are taking are conducive to living the life you want for yourself.

It would be difficult to end up in a rut if you were constantly following your heart, but most of us simply don't put that much thought into our everyday actions. However, our everyday actions add up. The little choices we make—or more importantly, fail to make—are what our lives are built of, so it helps to be aware of the choices you're making on a daily basis. You should also be extremely careful when making choices that affect your life on a daily basis, such as your job, location, spouse, and friends. If one of these things is not making you happy, then it will be extremely difficult to get out of your rut until you make a change.

In order to make decisions and take actions that will get you out of your rut, it is important to have a vision for your life. Which values do you consider to be the cornerstones of your life? Money? Family? Self-Expression? Adventure? When you wake up every morning, how do you want to feel? Motivated? Loved? Free? Excited? How do you want to make others feel? When you begin to carve out a vision for your life, the right life choices will become more obvious.

If you want to break free from the rut that you find yourself in, you will have to stop caring about what other people think. Do not be held back by what you feel society expects of you. If selling all your worldly possessions and backpacking around the world will make you happy, then don't let your business suits and your mortgage stop you. Put the house on the market and trade your suits in for jeans --if you truly feel that doing so will get you out of this endless cycle of discontentment. You don't have to care what your parents, co-workers, or peers think about it. It is vital that you base your decisions on what *you* want, not what others want for you. This may mean hurting some feelings or letting other people down, but that's okay. You will be a better son, daughter, mother, father, wife, husband, or friend if you feel happy and fulfilled.

Chapter 2: Shaking Things Up for Inspiration

One common symptom of being stuck in a rut is a lack of inspiration. You have been doing the same things, thinking the same things, and feeling the same things day after tiresome day. To break out of your rut, you need to break out of your routine. You need to do, think, and feel different things. Take a new route to work, go to a new restaurant, or try a new hairstyle. Doing things a little differently will help give you a new perspective.

Implement inspirational moments into your daily life. Get all five of your senses involved: Take a walk outside, listen to music, read a poem, or have a cup of coffee or tea. Herbal teas can help stir up the senses, and peppermint or rose petal teas are especially inspiring choices. Essential oils are also a great tool to provoke a new perspective. Inhale rosemary and/or peppermint to clear your head and kick-start your creativity, or experiment with different scents to discover which ones inspire you. Take the opportunity to shake things up and add variation and interest to your daily life. Not every change you make needs to be huge and life-altering. Adding these small inspirational moments to your day add up to make your life more fun and interesting.

Along with adding variation to your daily activities, you should enjoy an occasional adventure. Go to a concert or take a weekend camping trip. Call an old friend or a loved one. Any break from your usual routine will give you a fresh perspective. Too often do we tell ourselves that we are too busy to take a trip or go to an art exhibit. We think that those adventures will have to wait until next week, next month, or next year. We don't make those things a priority and forget about them, so we end up being just as busy next week, next month, and next year. And what are we so busy doing? Usually we are busy doing the things that make us feel bored, fatigued, and depressed. So carve out the time to be adventurous. Go to that concert tonight, and you will be more inspired at work tomorrow. Take that trip now, and you will be better able to tend to your responsibilities next week.

Another great way to get inspired is to simply talk to other people about whatever makes you feel stuck. You could speak generally about your lack of motivation and enthusiasm for life, or you could discuss more specific aspects of your lack of motivation. If you have trouble focusing on your paperwork, you might ask a co-worker for ideas about how to stay motivated to finish it. If you are having difficulties in your relationship, you might ask a trusted parent or friend for advice. Insight from other people is valuable, even if you don't end up following their suggestions. Merely thinking about things from another person's point of view will jump-start your own problem-solving skills. Of course, if you are feeling hopeless and are not sure where to turn for advice, it's always a good idea to talk with a professional therapist.

Chapter 3: Connecting with Your Physical Self

Sometimes, a psychological or emotional rut is often caused or exacerbated by a physical problem. Physical health has a direct and profound effect on emotional health, so it is important to get in tune with our bodies. A lack of motivation or an overarching sense of boredom may actually be fatigue caused by a sleep disorder, anemia, inadequate nutrition, a thyroid problem, diabetes, or some other underlying health issue. If you're not feeling great, you should consider seeing a doctor for a check-up and some testing. Additionally, there are things you can do on your own to promote physical health and well-being.

First, take nutrition seriously. What you eat certainly has an impact on your energy levels, and many studies show that nutrition has an effect on mood. So in order to break out of your rut and feel motivated again, you will want to implement a healthy diet. Cut out, or at least seriously limit, processed foods. You'll want to eat foods as close to their natural state as possible. For example, oatmeal is more natural than cold breakfast cereal and strawberries are more natural than strawberry-flavored ice cream. Ideally your diet would be made up entirely of whole foods, but packaged foods with only a handful of familiar ingredients are also a good choice. Foods in their natural state contain essential nutrients that your body and mind need in order to feel great and perform optimally, and they don't contain any additives or chemicals that might make you feel sick or tired. If you adopt a diet made up of natural foods for one week, I promise that you will notice a profound difference in your energy levels and your outlook on life.

Second, get some exercise. Exercise releases endorphins in the brain, promoting happiness and a general sense of well-being. Exercise can help you feel more energetic, which can boost your motivation and creativity. It doesn't have to be difficult or boring! Exercise can and should be fun. You don't have to pay a gym membership fee or spend countless hours on a treadmill to get exercise. You can go for a hike, play Frisbee in the park, or take your kids for a bike ride. A lot of folks' personal favorite form of exercise is to have a dance party, so turn on some fun music and dance to your heart's content! Find physical activities that *you* love to do and integrate them into your regular routine.

Last, be sure to take some time to relax. Our society is high-stress, and stress is toxic. A mind that has been in overdrive for too long is bound to start shutting down, causing you to fall into a rut. Take time every day to relax and clear your mind. You could try practicing meditation, taking a quiet walk outside, reading a book, having a glass of wine, or enjoying a bubble bath—do whatever works for you. Anything that helps you unwind from the stresses of your daily life will help you find your way out of your rut. A cluttered mind has no room for new thoughts and ideas, but a clear mind has room to dream, re-evaluate, and solve problems.

Chapter 4: How to Practice Positive Thinking

Positive thinking is a powerful tool to use when you are working toward breaking out of a rut. As we have discussed, a rut can lead to and can be perpetuated by depression. A hallmark symptom of depression is negative thinking, which can be an extremely difficult habit to change. Negative thinking is consuming and contagious—one negative thought leads to another and another, and all those negative thoughts make a situation seem much worse than it actually is. When you are stuck in a pattern of negative thinking, creativity and optimism are hindered. It becomes nearly impossible to generate solutions and possibilities for breaking free from the monotony of a rut. Practicing positive thinking will help make it possible for you to get motivated and inspired again.

Although you may feel silly doing it, repeating positive affirmations *out loud* on a regular basis is one of the most powerful ways to encourage positive thinking. If you have been struggling with writer's block, for instance, you might repeat the phrase "I am a wonderful writer; ideas and inspiration come easily to me." Or if you have been bored at work, you might use the phrase "I love my job; my work is exciting and important." Repeat the phrase every day before you begin your work, *especially* if you do not believe it to be true. The more you say it, the more you will think it, and these positive thoughts will eventually come to you automatically.

Visualization is another tool you can use to encourage a positive thought process. Close your eyes and imagine yourself typing away effortlessly. Imagine yourself at work, smiling, energetic, and happy to be there. Visualization helps train your mind to think that you are able to write effortlessly without end, or that you are always happy when you're at work. The more you visualize something, the more likely it is to become a reality.

Practicing gratitude is also a great way to increase your positive thoughts. You can make a list of things you are grateful for and hang it somewhere you can see it often, such as a bathroom mirror. Seeing your list every day will make you feel happy and will help promote positive thoughts. Alternatively, when you find yourself overtaken with a negative thought, you can combat it with something that makes you feel grateful. For example, "I hate my job" can become "I'm grateful to have a steady source of income." "My mother is so overbearing" can become "I'm lucky to have a mother that cares so much." Shifting your perspective in this way helps you see possibilities rather than obstacles.

The mind is an amazing thing. If you're aware of the concept of the placebo effect, you'll know that a person simply *thinking* that they'll get better greatly bolsters their chances of actually getting better. Never underestimate the power of your thoughts.

Chapter 5: Marching Forward with Small Steps

The strange thing about being in a rut is that you can be extremely bored and insanely overwhelmed at the same time: You are bored with your current circumstances, but you're overwhelmed regarding how to go about changing your life. When you are trying to get out of a rut, you should take small steps in order to avoid becoming disheartened. If you try to take on too much at once, you may become more overwhelmed and give up. It is better to take it slow and make steady improvements. Before you know it, you will be out of your rut and loving your life.

When I say take a small step, I mean *really* small. If you are feeling uninspired at work, start by clearing off and organizing your desk. Consider getting a plant for your cubicle. Then sit down at your clean, organized, and well-oxygenated desk and take the next step! If you are in a rut in your relationship, start small by implementing a weekly date night. It doesn't have to be fancy or elaborate; a simple dinner date will do, but be sure to focus on each other and enjoy some meaningful conversation. Make sure that each goal you set is attainable. Reaching your goals will encourage you to keep setting new ones. By taking these small steps, you can avoid feeling overwhelmed while still making changes that will help you move away from monotony.

If change seems to be coming about too slowly, be ready to counteract feeling discouraged. Keeping track of your progress might help you stay motivated. You could keep a journal or blog chronicling your journey. However, if journaling seems like another burden to take on, don't bother. If an activity does not inspire or motivate you, then don't pursue it. Again, you do not want to risk becoming overwhelmed. Just remember that no matter how small the next step you take is, it is still progress! Every step will get you a little bit closer to living the life you want.

Chapter 6: How to Be Accountable

For someone in a rut, it can be very difficult to stay motivated. You will need to take action to keep yourself accountable for the changes you are making. Otherwise, you are likely to abandon your goals and remain stagnant in life. To help yourself stay accountable, make your goals specific. General goals, such as "I want to live a more exciting life," are too difficult to keep track of. A better option might be "I want to take one new risk each week." Choose a goal that you could check off a list. Better yet, make an actual tangible list of your goals and check them off as you meet them. Many people respond well to a reward system. For each goal you meet or positive change you make, give yourself a reward. It could be something as simple as going out for ice cream. What is important is that you find a way to keep track of your progress and make sure you are reaching your goals.

Despite your best intentions, if you are in a rut, then you might not be the best person to keep yourself accountable for making any sort of progress. An uninspired person is very likely to give up at the slightest sign of difficulty. Instead of relying on your own motivation, which is in short supply during a rut, get someone else involved. Tell a friend, family member, or your spouse about the changes that you are making. Joining a group is another great way to stay accountable. If one of your goals is to be more creative, you could join a painting class. It would be even harder to skip if you had friends who were expecting to see you in class. However you go about it, make sure other people are aware of what you are up to. That way, you will be more likely to stick with the changes.

Conclusion

We all find ourselves unmotivated and bored once in a while. Ruts are a normal part of life. Nevertheless, when you do find yourself in a rut, you probably want to get out of it as soon as possible! A rut is not a fun place to be, and it is not always an easy place to escape from. You may not even know how you got there in the first place.

However, if you are self-aware, honest, patient, and determined, then you can break out of your rut and start living a life you love. With a little self-reflection, you can determine exactly what kind of life you want to live. This may apply to your job or a relationship, or it may apply to your whole life. Once you decide what you want, getting inspired and practicing positive thinking will help you start moving toward your goal. Don't forget to take care of yourself, because your physical health can have an effect on your emotional well-being. If you get too overwhelmed by all the changes you need to make, you can start by taking small steps. To help keep yourself accountable, tell a friend or family member about the changes you're making. If you are feeling too overwhelmed or extremely unmotivated, you may want to see your doctor. These could be symptoms of depression or another underlying medical condition.

Have fun in your journey, and try not to be too hard on yourself. Now is a great time to try things you have never tried before. Laugh, ask questions, take risks, and learn new things. If you can approach your life as an adventure, then it is not likely to be boring! Take life one day at a time, and before you know it you will be the happy, motivated, inspired person that you desire to be!

Finally, I'd like to thank you for purchasing this book! If you enjoyed it or found it helpful, I'd greatly appreciate it if you'd take a moment to leave a review on Amazon. Thank you!

Printed in Great Britain
by Amazon